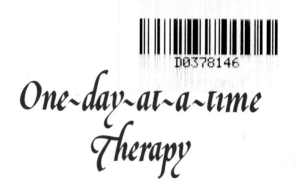

One~day~at~a~time
Therapy

One~day~at~a~time Therapy

written by
Christine A. Adams

illustrated by
R.W. Alley

ONE
CARING
PLACE
Abbey Press

Text © 1990 Christine A. Adams
Illustrations © 1990 St. Meinrad Archabbey
Published by One Caring Place
Abbey Press
St. Meinrad, Indiana 47577

Library of Congress Catalog Number
90-80719
ISBN 0-87029-228-5

Printed in the United States of America

Foreword

Do you feel stuck in the past? Do you repeatedly replay events that have already happened? Or do you find yourself projecting into the future, anticipating what hasn't yet happened—and may not. Preoccupation with remembering the past and projecting the future can keep you from living in the present.

The ability to live "in the moment" is one of the most important elements of life. It sounds simple; it is difficult to do.

One-day-at-a-time Therapy helps you to focus on today, to let go of painful memories of your past and your fears of the future. It encourages you to see yourself as a child, happy and loved and in control of your own life. It affirms that God is very close to you—and that God is *now!*

1.

You are never alone. The child within you is your steadfast companion.

2.

Notice your child within.
The child anticipates
your friendship.

3.

Protect your child within.
That child, like you, is
a child of God.

4.

Talk gently to your child within. The child needs your reassurance.

5.

Listen carefully to your child within. The child is wise.

6.

Do something special for your child within. You're never too old to play.

7.

Become aware of God's loving gaze. God takes special delight in you and in your child within.

8.

Be patient with your child
within. The child has
much to discover.

9.

When your child within misbehaves, do not scold. The child needs your gentle understanding.

10.

When your child within gets
lost, drugs, drink, sex,
or food won't help. Set
out to find your child again.

11.

When someone offends your child within, don't fight back. Wiping your child's tears is enough.

12.

Sing, hum, whistle. Your child within knows the tune.

13.

Notice the child within others.
Their child recognizes yours.

14.

Today, look at others as if you see them for the first time. You do.

15.

Become aware of all that
surrounds you at this moment.
God holds it all in existence.

16.

Receive the moment—and
all that are to come—as gift.
God is the unending Giver.

17.

Redecorate your life with God's gifts. Awe and wonder surround you.

18.

This moment is the only
moment you have.
Respect its possibilities.

19.

Celebrate the coincidences in
your life. They may be miracles.

20.

Today, let go of all expectations. God has a surprise for you.

21.

Acknowledge your own
remarkable goodness.
There is much to acknowledge.

22.

When something inside becomes painful today, ask yourself, "When did this pain begin?" It may be an old wound gradually healing.

23.

Just for today—just for a
moment—let go of hurtful
memories. There is peaceful
relief in letting go.

24.

Grab your fear of the future and ask, "What can I do about this right now?" You need not let fear control you.

ELF HAVEN HOME
FOR AGING ELVES

25.

When someone makes
you unhappy, pause.
Remember: only you
can make you unhappy.

26.

When you feel unloved,
give love away. It will
come back to you.

27.

Do not attempt to control
others. Control stifles freedom.

28.

Never hold anything too tight.
To cling is to suffocate.

29.

Keep it simple. Only do today
what you can do today.

30.

When life becomes
boring, risk! You'll discover
the wonders of your
own courage.

31.

When you see something broken,
fix it. You are capable.

32.

When you see something
working, leave it alone.
Enjoy it; you're entitled.

33.

Today, love and forgive.
That's all you need to do —
one day at a time.

34.

If today seems shrouded in hopelessness, pray. Let go and let God.

35.

Regardless of what this
day brings, thank God.
An untouched day
awaits you tomorrow.

Christine A. Adams is a writer and teacher. She is the author of the Abbey Press book *Claiming Your Own Life—As the Adult Child of an Alcoholic* and a number of Abbey Press *CareNotes,* as well as *Living in Love: Connecting to the Power of Love Within* (Health Communications, Inc.). She lives in Connecticut and has three grown children.

Illustrator for the Abbey Press Elf-help Books, **R.W. Alley** also illustrates and writes children's books. He lives in Barrington, Rhode Island, with his wife, daughter, and son.

The Story of the Abbey Press Elves

The engaging figures that populate the Abbey Press "elf-help" line of publications and products first appeared in 1987 on the pages of a small self-help book called *Be-good-to-yourself Therapy*. Shaped by the publishing staff's vision and defined in R.W. Alley's inventive illustrations, they lived out author Cherry Hartman's gentle, self-nurturing advice with charm, poignancy, and humor.

Reader response was so enthusiastic that more Elf-help Books were soon under way, a still-growing series that has inspired a line of related gift products.

The especially endearing character featured in the early books—sporting a cap with a mood-changing candle in its peak—has since been joined by a spirited female elf with flowers in her hair.

These two exuberant, sensitive, resourceful, kindhearted, lovable sprites, along with their lively elfin community, reveal what's truly important as they offer messages of joy and wonder, playfulness and co-creation, wholeness and serenity, the miracle of life and the mystery of God's love.

With wisdom and whimsy, these little creatures with long noses demonstrate the elf-help way to a rich and fulfilling life.

Elf-help Books

...adding "a little character" and a lot
of help to self-help reading!

Grieving at Christmastime   #20052

Elf-help for Giving the Gift of You!   #20054

Grief Therapy (new, revised edition)   #20178

Healing Thoughts for Troubled Hearts   #20058

Take Charge of Your Eating   #20064

Elf-help for Coping With Pain   #20074

Elf-help for Dealing with Difficult People   #20076

Loneliness Therapy   #20078

Elf-help for Healing from Divorce   #20082

Music Therapy   #20083

'Tis a Blessing to Be Irish   #20088

Getting Older, Growing Wiser   #20089

Worry Therapy   #20093

Elf-help for Raising a Teen   #20102

Elf-help for Being a Good Parent   #20103

Gratitude Therapy   #20105

Trust-in-God Therapy	#20119
Elf-help for Overcoming Depression	#20134
New Baby Therapy	#20140
Teacher Therapy	#20145
Stress Therapy	#20153
Making-sense-out-of-suffering Therapy	#20156
Get Well Therapy	#20157
Anger Therapy	#20127
Caregiver Therapy	#20164
Self-esteem Therapy	#20165
Peace Therapy	#20176
Friendship Therapy	#20174
Christmas Therapy (color edition) $5.95	#20175
Happy Birthday Therapy	#20181
Forgiveness Therapy	#20184
Keep-life-simple Therapy	#20185
Acceptance Therapy	#20190
Keeping-up-your-spirits Therapy	#20195
Slow-down Therapy	#20203

One-day-at-a-time Therapy #20204

Prayer Therapy #20206

Be-good-to-your-marriage Therapy #20205

Be-good-to-yourself Therapy #20255

Book price is $4.95 unless otherwise noted.
Available at your favorite giftshop or bookstore—
or directly from One Caring Place, Abbey Press
Publications, St. Meinrad, IN 47577.
Or call 1-800-325-2511.
www.carenotes.com